The Name-Game

A Program About Inappropriate Behavior For Students In Grades One Through Four

by

Timothy G. Ludwig

illustrated by

Harry Norcross

About The Author

Tim Ludwig has been a counselor/educator for the past twenty years, working on all levels—kindergarten through post-secondary. Since 1982 he has been employed as a counselor at North Plains Elementary School, Minot Air Force Base, North Dakota. During this time, he has given numerous presentations and has conducted a variety of workshops at local and state conferences. He has also served as president of the North Dakota School Counselor Association. He and his wife, Cheryl, have one son, Kyle.

Published by
mar•co products, inc.
1443 Old York Road
Warminster, PA 18974

Library of Congress Catalog Card Number: 94-077202

ISBN: 1-884063-21-7

Printed in the U.S.A.

The Name-Game

The Name-Game is a story that teaches students the pitfalls of common misbehaviors. It tells of a boy named Willie who acts up and misbehaves to get attention. He acts weird, tattles, steals, lies, bullies, and dresses sloppily. The other students respond by calling him names. It is a story which can be used as a preventative lesson for those students who may someday try these types of behaviors and as a corrective lesson for those students exhibiting these behaviors. The story can be completed in one lesson or expanded into several lessons.

Each misbehavior, Willie tries, can be used as a lesson in itself. There are seven misbehaviors and one culminating lesson in which Willie realizes that he should be himself and eliminate the misbehaviors from his actions. Each misbehavior is introduced with a short story about Willie and his behavior. Following the story are discussion questions which will give the students an opportunity to further explore the misbehavior and make some decisions about themselves and others. The leader may choose to discuss one or more behaviors at each session. Allow about ten to fifteen minutes to fully discuss each misbehavior.

If the story is to be completed in one lesson, the leader should select only a few of the questions from each misbehavior before reading the story. This is necessary because the available number of questions for each misbehavior are too many to be used in only one session.

At the end of the story, there are several activity sheets. These may be reproduced for the students and used at the leader's discretion.

NAME-CALLING (PAGE 28)

Reproduce a copy of the *Name-Calling* activity sheet for each student. Tell the students to look at the pictures of Willie and to look at the list of words. Ask them to draw a line from the word to the picture it describes. When finished, discuss the students' answers.

FIND THE SECRET MESSAGE (PAGE 29)

Reproduce a copy of the *Find The Secret Message* activity sheet for each student. Tell the students to cross out all of the letters B, C, J, K, Q, R, S, V, X, and Z. Have them take the remaining letters and write them in the blank spaces provided. When they have finished, they will see the secret message. The message is "If You Don't Want The Name, Don't Play The Game."

WHAT DO YOU THINK WILL HAPPEN? (PAGE 30)

Reproduce a copy of the *What Do You Think Will Happen?* activity sheet for each student. Read the situation together. Then, ask the students to draw what they think the boys will do. When finished, have the students share their drawings.

ACTION WHEEL (PAGE 31)

Reproduce a copy of the *Action Wheel* activity for each student. Tell the students that they will hear several situations. Have them listen to the situations, decide which of the actions on the Action Wheel they would do in each situation, and then write the number of the situation somewhere in the space that matches the action they chose. Explain to the students that there may be other actions they would take, but these are the only four from which they can choose. The leader should then read the following situations:

1. A classmate comes to school with oatmeal on his shirt and a milk ring around his mouth. As he gets closer, it is obvious he hasn't taken a bath recently or brushed his teeth. He wants to sit with you at lunch. What action toward the student would you take?

2. A classmate is caught stealing your lunch money from your desk. What action toward the student would you take?

3. You are waiting in line for a drink at the water fountain. A classmate comes up to you and pushes in front of you. What action toward the student would you take?

4. The teacher comes over to you and asks you why you called a classmate a name. Everyone was joking around and calling names when this happened. What action toward the student would you take?

5. A classmate is telling you about how great she is. No matter what you have done, she has done it better. What action toward the student would you take?

6. You are on the school bus riding home. Every night, this one particular boy yells and bangs on the seat. Tonight he is sitting behind you. What action toward the student would you take?

7. In your class there is one girl who is always making noises. Whenever the teacher starts to teach, this girl lets out a loud noise of some kind and the teachers stops teaching and scolds her. What action toward the student would you take?

When finished, discuss the students' choices.

BOOKMARKS (PAGE 32)

Reproduce the bookmarks on heavy paper and cut them out. Distribute them to the students at various times to use in their library or text books. These bookmarks will help them keep track of the page they are on and remind them to avoid the misbehaviors they have learned about.

Acting Weird

One day at school, Willie thought he would be funny and make the other kids laugh...so he broke a pencil in half and stuck the ends in his ears.

Then, he crossed his eyes, made funny noises, jumped around, and just plain acted "weird."

Well, the other kids did laugh. But they weren't laughing *with* Willie, they were laughing *at* him.

"Boy, Willie, you are one *weird* kid," said one girl.

"Yeah, really *strange*!" said another.

"Hey everybody, stay away from Willie. He's a weirdo!"

"Willie is a Weirdo, Willie is a Weirdo."

That night, Willie couldn't sleep.

All he could think about was that horrible name which the other kids had called him in school that day, and it made him cry.

IF YOU DON'T WANT THE NAME-DON'T PLAY THE GAME!

Questions For Discussion

1. What name was Willie called? *(Weirdo.)*

2. Why did the kids call him that name? *(Because he did things that the other kids in the class did not do, like sticking pencil ends in his ears, crossing his eyes, making funny noises, and jumping around.)*

3. Did the other kids laugh with Willie or laugh at him? *(At him.)* What is the difference? *(Laughing with someone means that everyone is laughing together. Laughing at someone means you are making fun or singling that person out as weird or different.)*

4. What game was Willie playing? *(If I do strange things, the kids will notice me, laugh at me, and pay attention to me.)*

5. What could Willie have done differently? *(Stop acting strangely and start doing positive things that the other kids would notice.)*

6. Would you like to act like Willie? *(Accept any reasonable answers.)* Why? or Why not? *(Accept any reasonable answers.)*

7. What do you think you could say, to a kid acting like Willie, to help him/her understand that his/her behavior is inappropriate? *(Accept any reasonable answers.)*

8. What game was Willie playing? *(Acting weird.)*

Tattling

Willie was eating an ice-cream cone in the school lunchroom when Jack bumped into him, causing the cone to fall to the floor.

"You did that on purpose, Jack!" Willie yelled, and with that, he ran off to tell the teacher.

As a result, Jack had to stay for an hour after school that day.

Willie suddenly realized a new sense of power. "I can get the other kids into a whole lot of trouble by telling the teacher if they do something bad."

And that is just what he did. He even told the teacher if he *thought* they did something wrong. It got to the point where he was spending more time at the teacher's desk tattling than at his own desk working.

"You're nothing but a big tattletale, Willie!" said one of his classmates. "And half the time we haven't done any of the things you tell the teacher!"

"Nobody wants a tattletale for a friend."

"Willie is a Tattletale. Willie is a Tattletale."

That night, Willie couldn't sleep.

All he could think about was that horrible name which the other kids had called him in school that day, and it made him cry.

IF YOU DON'T WANT THE NAME-DON'T PLAY THE GAME!

Questions For Discussion

1. What did the kids call Willie? *(Tattletale.)*

2. What did Willie do to get called this name? *(He told the teacher about everything he thought the other kids were doing. Sometimes what he said was true and sometimes it was not.)*

3. Why did Willie start tattling on everyone? *(After he did it once, he realized that tattling made him feel powerful.)*

4. What game was Willie playing? *(If I tell on the other kids and get them in trouble then I will be powerful and in control.)*

5. What happens when someone tattles about every little thing to the teacher? *(They lose friends and are not respected by others.)*

6. What could Willie have done differently so he wouldn't be called a "Tattletale?" *(Stop telling the teacher about every little thing he thought the kids were doing. Accept any reasonable answers.)*

7. Are there times when it is good to tell? *(Yes, tattling is when someone tells about little problems like pushing in line or being bumped into. But, telling is for big problems like being in dangerous situations.)*

8. Would you like to act like Willie? *(Accept any reasonable answers.)* Why? or Why not? *(Accept any reasonable answers.)*

9. What do you think you could say, to a kid acting like Willie, to help him/her understand that his/her behavior is inappropriate? *(Accept any reasonable answers.)*

10. What game was Willie playing? *(Tattling.)*

Stealing

One morning, Willie *borrowed* a ruler from one of his classmates, but forgot to return it.

Later that day, he *found* a quarter on the teacher's desk. "Finder's keepers, loser's weepers!" he said to himself.

Still later that day, he took one of Susan Clark's pencils. "I think she once took one of mine, so it's only fair," he thought.

Soon, all of his classmates started hiding their things whenever he came around.

"Watch out for Willie. He's a little thief," everyone would say.

"Yeah, you just can't trust Willie!"

"Willie is a Stealer. Willie is a Stealer."

That night, Willie couldn't sleep.

All he could think about was that horrible name which the other kids had called him in school that day, and it made him cry.

IF YOU DON'T WANT THE NAME-DON'T PLAY THE GAME!

Questions For Discussion

1. What name did Willie get called? *(Stealer.)*

2. What did he do to get called this name? *(He took other people's things.)*

3. What happens to adults when they steal and get caught by the police? *(They may go to jail or get fined.)*

4. How do you feel when someone steals something from you? *(Accept any reasonable answers.)*

5. Do you think Willie will have friends if he steals from the other kids? Why? or Why not? *(No, because kids won't trust him and will want to keep away from him.)*

6. How does Willie need to change his behavior? *(He needs to stop taking other people's things.)*

7. Would you like to act like Willie? *(Accept any reasonable answers.)* Why? or Why not? *(Accept any reasonable answers.)*

8. What do you think you could say, to a kid acting like Willie, to help him/her understand that his/her behavior is inappropriate? *(Accept any reasonable answers.)*

9. What game was Willie playing? *(Stealing.)*

Talking Loudly

Willie once got the idea in his head that he wasn't getting enough attention in school. "I'll make sure *everyone* knows I'm around," he said to himself.

Well, that day Willie was *very* loud.

He ran around making all kinds of racket. He was the loudest voice in the halls, in the bathrooms, and in the lunchroom.

In the classroom, he was not only loud, but rude. Whenever the teacher would ask a question, he would bang his desk and shout out the answers even when it wasn't his turn.

"Quiet, Willie!" the other kids finally said.

"Give your mouth a rest, Willie."

"What a big mouth!"

"Big Mouth. Big Mouth. Willie is a Big Mouth."

That night, Willie couldn't sleep.

All he could think about was that horrible name which the other kids had called him in school that day, and it made him cry.

IF YOU DON'T WANT THE NAME-DON'T PLAY THE GAME!

Questions For Discussion

1. What was Willie called? *(Big Mouth.)*

2. How did he get this name? *(He was loud everywhere, shouted out answers, and was rude.)*

3. What do you think about someone with a "big mouth"? *(Accept any reasonable answers.)*

4. How could Willie change his behavior so he would be accepted and liked by the other kids? *(By talking quietly, taking turns answering, and not shouting out.)*

5. Would you like to act like Willie? *(Accept any reasonable answers.)* Why? or Why not? *(Accept any reasonable answers.)*

6. What do you think you could say, to a kid acting like Willie, to help him/her understand that his/her behavior is inappropriate? *(Accept any reasonable answers.)*

7. What game was Willie playing? *(Notice me. He did this by being loud, talking out, and not taking turns answering.)*

Being Sloppy And Dirty

One day Willie came to school looking like he'd just fallen off a hay wagon. His clothes were all dirty, his hair was a tangled mess, and half of his breakfast was still on his chin. And because he looked such a mess, the kids started calling him a "Sloppy Joe."

"Willie is a Sloppy Joe, Sloppy Joe," they called out.

"I can't help it if my parents can't afford new clothes for me," he told them. But the other kids knew that you don't need to have new clothes to look neat. Even old clothes can look fine if they are kept clean.

And Willie could look downright handsome if only he would remember to wash his face, comb his hair, and brush his teeth before he came to school in the morning.

"Willie is a Sloppy Joe, Sloppy Joe."

That night, Willie couldn't sleep.

All he could think about was that horrible name which the other kids had called him in school that day, and it made him cry.

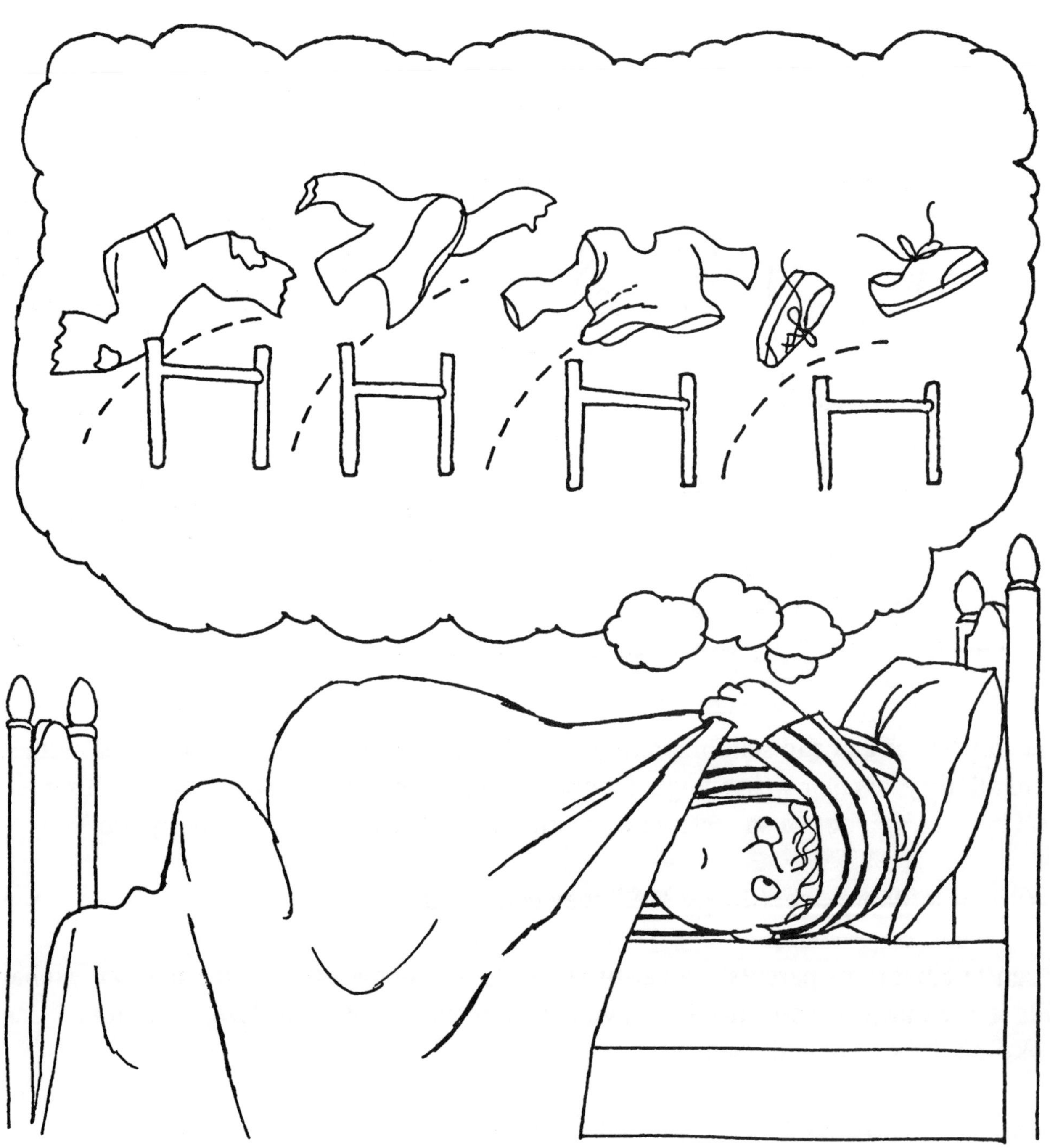

IF YOU DON'T WANT THE NAME-DON'T PLAY THE GAME!

Questions For Discussion

1. What name was Willie called? *(Sloppy Joe.)*

2. What did Willie do to be called this name? *(Wore dirty clothes, didn't comb his hair, didn't wash his hands and face, etc.)*

3. Do you ever forget to do some of these things? How do you feel? *(Accept any reasonable answers.)*

4. What could Willie have done so the kids wouldn't call him "Sloppy Joe"? (*Washed himself, brushed his teeth, worn clean clothes, combed his hair, etc.)*

5. Would you like to act like Willie? *(Accept any reasonable answers.)* Why? or Why not? *(Accept any reasonable answers.)*

6. What do you think you could say, to a kid acting like Willie, to help him/her understand that his/her behavior is inappropriate? *(Accept any reasonable answers.)*

7. What game was Willie playing? *(It's not my fault that I am not clean.)*

Lying

Willie realized he wasn't having the best of luck making friends, so he sat down and started thinking about things he could do to get other kids to like him. "I know," he thought to himself. "I'll tell them things that will *really* impress them." So he started bragging.

Everything about Willie was either faster, bigger, or better than anyone else's. Or at least Willie told everyone so.

But most of the kids knew that Willie was just making everything up. He really didn't have or do any of those things he was bragging about.

"Oh, Willie, you're just making that stuff up!" they said.

"You are just telling a big bunch of lies!"

"Yeah, you can't believe anything he says!" they cried.

"Liar. Liar. Willie is a Liar!"

That night, Willie couldn't sleep.

All he could think about was that horrible name which the other kids had called him in school that day, and it made him cry.

IF YOU DON'T WANT THE NAME-DON'T PLAY THE GAME!

Questions For Discussion

1. What name was Willie called? *(Liar.)*
2. What did Willie do to get called this name? *(He exaggerated and bragged about things that were not true.)*
3. Why did Willie tell things that weren't true? *(He wanted to impress the kids so they would like him.)*
4. Have you ever tried to impress someone by bragging or telling things that weren't true? *(Accept any reasonable answers.)*
5. How do you feel about someone who is always talking about how great he/she is? *(Accept any reasonable answers.)*
6. How could Willie change his behavior so he wouldn't be called a liar? *(Tell the truth. Not brag or exaggerate to impress people.)*
7. Would you like to act like Willie? *(Accept any reasonable answers.)* Why? or Why not? *(Accept any reasonable answers.)*
8. What do you think you could say, to a kid acting like Willie, to help him/her understand that his/her behavior is inappropriate? *(Accept any reasonable answers.)*
9. What game was Willie playing? *(If you think I'm really great, you will like me.)*

Bullying

Willie decided that he was tired of being pushed around and being called names.

"From now on, I'm going to do all the pushing and teasing!" he thought to himself.

Not only did Willie push and tease, but he also shoved, kicked, punched, and bullied his way through the day.

He shoved a little girl out of a swing because he wanted it; he kicked over a boy's desk just to be mean; he punched another boy in the stomach because he wanted to be first in the lunch line; and he bullied a little kindergarten girl into carrying his books for him.

"You've turned into such a bully," said one of his former friends.

"Yeah, you've gotten to be so mean, who would want to hang around with you?"

"You're a Bully, Willie—Mean, Mean, Mean!"

That night, Willie couldn't sleep.

All he could think about was that horrible name which the other kids had called him in school that day, and it made him cry.

IF YOU DON'T WANT THE NAME-DON'T PLAY THE GAME!

Questions For Discussion

1. What name did the kids call Willie? *(Bully.)*

2. What did Willie do when he was tired of being called names and being pushed around? *(Pushed, teased, shoved, kicked, punched, and became a bully.)*

3. Do you know any bullies? What do they do? How do you feel about a bully? *(Accept any reasonable answers.)*

4. Have you ever been a bully? What did you do? How did other kids treat you? *(Accept any reasonable answers.)*

5. What could Willie have done differently so he wouldn't have been called a bully? *(Stop shoving, teasing, pushing, and threatening the other kids)*

6. Would you like to act like Willie? *(Accept any reasonable answers.)* Why? or Why not? *(Accept any reasonable answers.)*

7. What do you think you could say, to a kid acting like Willie, to help him/her understand that his/her behavior is inappropriate? *(Accept any reasonable answers.)*

8. What game was Willie playing? *(I'll get what I want by being mean and bullying others.)*

Willie Wises Up

Today, Willie didn't play any games. He wasn't a tattletale. He wasn't a weirdo. He wasn't a stealer. He wasn't a big mouth. He wasn't a Sloppy Joe. He wasn't even a braggart or a meanie. He was just himself—Willie.

He didn't play any games and he wasn't called any names, but one—Willie.

AND TONIGHT HE IS GOING TO GET A GOOD NIGHT'S SLEEP!

Questions For Discussion

1. How do you think Willie felt being himself? *(Good.)*

2. How do you think the other kids felt about Willie when he behaved just as himself? *(Accept any reasonable answers.)*

3. What game was Willie playing? *(None.)*

4. Did Willie learn a valuable lesson? *(Yes.)*

5. What can we learn from the story about Willie? *(Be yourself and treat others the way you would like to be treated.)*

Name-Calling

Name ____

Look at the pictures of Willie. He is doing all the things that made the kids call him names. Then, look at the list of names. Match the picture to the name by drawing a line from the name to its matching picture.

Sloppy Joe

Bully

Weirdo

Stealer

Tattletale

Big Mouth

Liar

Find The Secret Message

Name ____

Look at all the letters below. Cross out every B C J K Q R S V X Z.

S I B F C Q Y O S K U J D J O

R C N V T Z W B A N J T K Q

T R X H Z E N B A C S M V E

J D V O C K N B T R P Q L J

X Z A C Y Q T R H V E S G

R C A J M Z V R E

Put the letters left from above in the blanks and read the message.

__ __   __ __ __   __ __ __' __

__ __ __ __   __ __ __   __ __ __ __,

__ __ __' __   __ __ __ __

__ __ __   __ __ __ __.

What Do You Think Will Happen?

Name ____

Willie wanted everyone to think he was the best baseball player in the room. He told all the other boys how well he had done on a team last year. He told them he had been the pitcher and that the coach wanted him to pitch all the games, but gave the other guys a chance only because he had to. He also told them that he was the best hitter on the team. Some of the boys in his class were on his team last year and knew Willie wasn't telling the truth. Draw a picture of what you think the other boys will do when Willie wants to play baseball with them.

Action Wheel

Name ____

Write the number of the situation read in the section of the Action Wheel that shows what you would do.

Bookmarks

KEEP
YOURSELF
NEAT
&
CLEAN

Lying
and
Stealing
Hurts
Others
and
You!

IF YOU
DON'T
WANT THE
NAME...
DON'T
PLAY THE
GAME!